CREMATING PAST

The Spirit's Destiny II

CARLOS MEDINA

Copyright © 2018 by **Carlos Medina**

All rights reserved. No part of this publication may be reproduced, distributed or transmitted in any form or by any means, without prior written permission.

Carlos Medina / Magesoul Publishing
PO BOX 580019
Bronx, NY 10458
www.magesoul.com

Publisher's Note: This is a work of fiction. Names, characters, places, and incidents are a product of the author's imagination. Locales and public names are sometimes used for atmospheric purposes. Any resemblance to actual people, living or dead, or to businesses, companies, events, institutions, or locales is completely coincidental.

Edited by Soshinie A. Singh
Book Cover © 2018 Nour Tohamy

Bulk purchases from Magesoul Publishing are available with discounts.

Cremating Past / Carlos Medina -- 1st ed.
ISBN 978-0-9980403-0-1

DEDICATION

To everyone who has walked through the grave of their past, and to those who are still struggling to find the exit: this is for your strength.

FOREWORD

Carlos Medina is a very powerful writer. He manages to shake you with his simple words which an also sink deep into your bones.

- Soshinie Singh, Editor

I failed many times in my life. But within those failures I found strength. Though it took me many years and a divorce to truly understand that it all had to happen the way it did. I went into a relationship to try and help a broken soul. My intention was never to hurt the person. But back then, I believed that within the needs of two individuals, love can grow. When in reality, it always takes two individuals to love each other, for the love to keep going. I look back now and see all the signs that it wouldn't last. My mistake was trying to help a person and falling for her outer appearance. I fell for her character. That's a weak point for a Scorpio. When we see a female take charge or initiative in a relationship - We crumble. She loved the power I had, in business and personal life. But here is the thing. What happens when a soul is no longer broken? They leave. They leave thinking that they can handle life on their own. And probably most could. And some can't. So, when you fall in love with someone. Make sure it's felt within. On both sides. Make sure it's not ONLY out of need. You'll feel it. Trust me. You'll know when they are the one. Your mind will declare war on your soul. So, allow the heart to be the referee. And watch the magic happen.

Why did I fail in my past?
I just wasn't able to bring the illusion to reality.
But now, I don't only show you an illusion, I can also make it a reality.
Above all, now I can allow you to feel my soul.

CREMATING PAST

You must be willing to let go of your past, take time to heal and trust in the process. Love sometimes comes in unexplainable ways. But it definitely comes.

She was willing to let go, just for a taste of what she deserved.

CREMATING PAST

If my love can make you forget the pain from your past, then I know that I have been successful in reaching the depths of my soul.

It's hard to see what the future can bring when the past keeps haunting her mind daily. Losing hope was never a choice for she knew that deep inside her, she had the strength to keep going.

CREMATING PAST

Many daggers have been thrown at my heart from my past. Many times I have been belittled. My spirit was left in solitude in hopes that I would destroy myself within my deep emotions. I had just forgotten that within me I have all the powers to destroy myself a million times until the right me is ready to rise.

It was hard to believe again, to feel again and to love again. But she knew life couldn't be lived without love. Her past was really painful but she promised herself that she would do everything possible to make her future bright. She knew it was a sacrifice, but it was a sacrifice well worth it.

CREMATING PAST

Are you willing to let go of all your past?
If so, just take my hand and allow me to show you the love you always deserved.

Pain will make you stop believing. It will close the door to your soul. It will break your heart. But you cannot allow it to destroy parts of your future. Give yourself time to heal. But allow yourself to be loved the way you deserve.

CREMATING PAST

He made a mess of your beauty. I'm willing to take that mess and cherish its hidden beauty.

Many thought she was done. They thought she wouldn't get back up. In their minds, she was done. She knew that's not the way it was going to end. She believed in herself. She found courage to do it again. To burn. To rise. To demonstrate that nothing will stop her.

CREMATING PAST

Maybe you weren't special to them. But in the eyes of a pure soul, you're everything.

I wasn't always the person I am today. I was the person everyone expected me to be. For many years, I lived hidden inside my darkness. I knew one day those chains would break. I knew one day I would be free. That day came, and here I am exposing my all to the world. I am showcasing what was hidden for so long.

CREMATING PAST

It's ok. It's not the end of the world. Love comes, and love goes. Love hurts but it also heals. Feelings come and they will go. But one thing is for sure, what's yours will remain. In good or bad. No matter the obstacles or rough patches. If they go, let them. They were just a lesson in life. And if they decide to stay and be a part of your future, cherish them. Work together through it all. Be united as one. It's a beautiful thing when two souls have the same goals in life. It's the beginning of generations to come.

Strap my thoughts around your heart and smile, for my soul has orchestrated a rainbow for you.

CREMATING PAST

Take a good grip of my heart, for my soul is ready to elevate you.

There comes a time when you just don't know what's happiness anymore. You forget what it is that you deserve, desire and hope for. We feel like this life is just a game. We feel like puppets waiting for the moment when someone comes along and cuts the string that attaches us to our past. We live daily crying those invincible tears into the night, hoping that somehow, the moon decides to bring us some light within. It hurts more knowing, that some people do settle for mediocre, because they've given up on fate. They've given up on that pure love.

CREMATING PAST

Life is full of many lessons, surprises, pain, suffering, mistakes and love. Sometimes when we give up, we were real close to our turning point. Nothing in this life is easy. Take it one step at a time and breathe. Have patience and believe that everything is unfolding the way it's meant to be.

Why would I want to go back to the past?
There's so much beauty in my future.

CREMATING PAST

My entire life I lived with stolen wings from an angel. Clipping them off was the only way to cut that cord that attached me to the past. It took two years and three deaths of myself to actually earn the ones I carry today. How could anyone dare to think I would be stupid enough to go back to the old me?

Let's lay all our troubles to rest. Slowly, let's defeat the shadows that follow us from our past. Together let's see our future from the eyes of the unknown.

CREMATING PAST

I always wondered, if you were actually my home. I thought that you by my side was actually the safest place to be. Physically and mentally I was safe. I was in no need of anything materialistic because I had you. But somehow I felt empty. My whole inside felt the solitude of a soul walking in a desert. It's crazy to think, you could have so many things in this life and still feel alone, empty and abandoned. I recall every moment where I tried to talk to you and fix things, where I tried so hard to express to you how vacant I felt inside. All I got in return was, "you need help, you're going crazy and you're seeing things that are not there." Thinking about it now, I was seeing things that weren't there. My soul kept wishing for a love that didn't exist between us. See, from birth I've been searching for this deep connection. A connection that stands against all the winds, all the hatred and all the evil that resides in this cynical world.

The day you walked into my life, is when I knew I had to call my past and thank her for the beautiful lesson learned.

CREMATING PAST

Being in love is your soul yearning to be in the presence of its other. It's counting the minutes until you are finally home within the other. It's dreaming of them and knowing that once you wake up, they are your reality. It's not thinking about your past anymore but thinking about the future with them by your side. Being in love, is flying with their wings and knowing that you won't fall.

When you begin to see things through your soul, your eyes will see things differently from that point on. You will understand what's fabricated from the mind and what's illuminated by the soul.

CREMATING PAST

Her heart will forgive you, her soul will never forget.

I distanced myself from the past just to find you. I brought you into my writing just to open your mind and show you the beauty you hold. I surrendered my soul to you in the middle of the night, just to keep you safe during the lonely times.

CREMATING PAST

To love again, you must kill your old self.

I watched you while you were sleeping, and the only thing that crossed my mind was, what are we doing here? When you and I know that this isn't working the way we thought it would. I knew our time was coming to an end. I knew it, but couldn't do anything about it. I couldn't make up the lost time. I couldn't take back all the words that were never meant to come out. I just simply couldn't say, I love you with all my soul.

CREMATING PAST

Trust in your gut feeling,
It's fucking powerful.

It's not that she gave up on the relationship, it's just been all the little things that you didn't pay attention to that made her walk away for self respect.

CREMATING PAST

For your love, I'll cremate my old self. I'll frame my soul and showcase it to the world. I'll clip my wings and hand them to you, just to assure you that there is power in love. Above all things mentioned, I will make sure you feel my presence daily. You will feel my unconditional love and finally understand, that ancient souls still exist.

I come before you to surrender my soul. I recognize that the love I have within was desired by you lifetimes ago. So take all the shattered pieces of my heart and create that masterpiece that lasts forever.

CREMATING PAST

I always thought that holding on to you would give us the strength we needed to keep going. To forget all our bad moments, and hopefully create new ones. But it was all the complete opposite. The more I held on to you, the more I lost myself. I lost myself in all your darkness. I couldn't continue trying to rescue us by myself. I just couldn't keep up the fake smiles any longer. I had to walk away. I had to leave what we had, because it turned to what you wanted instead of what we wanted.

It's never one thing that will hurt us. It's all the little things accumulating that hurts us the most. It's constantly reminding the person that gets to us. And it gets tiring after a while.

CREMATING PAST

I'm not like the rest. I can assure you that. What many failed on, I will succeed. What many hide inside, I bring out to light from within. Yes! I'm that ancient soul that suffocates your heart with love. The one that many can't handle.

Don't give me that bullshit - hey babe kind of love. Give me that deep passionate - I want to make love to your soul until I destroy your past, kind of love.

CREMATING PAST

One night, I screamed real loud. I was hoping that you would hear me. I was praying and begging the almighty for you to open up your eyes. I prayed that for once, just once, you could actually hear me, that you could understand how much pain I have inside of me. But you didn't. You didn't care for us, you only cared for yourself. I truly felt alone for the first time in my life. How can it be? A person in a relationship and still feel so alone. How can this be, to give your whole heart to a person, and somehow still live neglected by that same person. I truly did love you. But I love myself more.

One day, you woke up and everything made sense. You finally understood that to find your soul, you had to let go.

CREMATING PAST

It will take time. It will take your heart to align with your soul. But I promise you this, you will learn to love again. Just this time, it will be with more knowledge and depth.

One day it will all make sense, the pain, the suffering and the heartbreak. You will look back and realize what a masterpiece was created.

CREMATING PAST

And when it's all over, you have no other choice but to move on. It doesn't matter what you do. If they don't feel the same way towards you, it will be a waste of time to try to rekindle something that has no hope. Yes I know, the time invested in the relationship is time you will never get back. But you have to keep moving forward. Take this time to work on yourself. Do the things you always imagined doing. Go out and pamper yourself. Go to sleep late. Drink from that bottle that you always wanted to drink from. Go to the movies. Go and have some fun with your friends. Don't try to fall into another relationship quickly. Take care of your soul first. Once it feels that the time is right, you'll know and feel that special someone. You will no longer smile to hide pain, you'll smile, for someone beautiful has made you smile. You'll smile because they are in your thoughts. You will feel that powerful presence. Forget about feeling the butterflies, you'll feel all your insides wanting to come out. For once in your life, you'll feel your soul wanting to scream, THIS IS PURE LOVE!

I apologized to you every time that I or you did something wrong. You never accepted them, because you didn't really care about us. When I decided to walk away, that was the first time you actually heard me. Unfortunately, it was the last time you heard my voice.

CREMATING PAST

It took me years to heal from my past pain. Killing my old self was just a way for me to reincarnate as the soul I am today. Tuning into you was my way of absorbing all your pain. Touching your soul was my way of showing you that pure love still exist. Whispering every night into your thoughts was the greatest example that I lived by my words. Falling for you daily, was just me showcasing my soul to you and assuring you, that our eternity is well within our depths.

Everything you lost will fade away once you open your eyes to what's hidden within you.

CREMATING PAST

Once again, you abandoned me. You kept me in the stage of hope, visualizing our future as one. I thought the third time would be a charm, but the reality is, you're still the same person I meet two years ago. You're still stuck in the " I can't believe this is happening mode". You're still hesitant to what beauty could rise from these ashes I have crawled through. It's even more crazy to know that I still feel the same for you, that I still believe in something that I felt from the first time I laid eyes on you. What many consider a torture, a curse, I consider it as a blessing. It's a blessing to feel these things deeply, to see things differently and to continue having hope although many people try to take it away. It's a blessing to know, that the love I have inside can break many internal barriers and bypass all the mental chambers that create illusions and obstacles. This type of love, this type of love comes from many painful events and a lot of tears. It's rare and pure. It's a beautiful blessing to feel the things that I never thought existed in me.

It felt like home. But I knew my stay wasn't for long.

CREMATING PAST

I remember it so clearly, that night when you fell asleep and I heard the ringtone of a message from your phone. The first thing that crossed my mind was that your boss was being an asshole and wanted you to go in and cover someone's shift. But for some reason, I felt something different, I felt that something was not right. Once I heard the second ring, I knew that I had to lift that phone up. I knew deep down inside, that this was not good. Seeing all those notifications gave me the worst feelings. I felt for the first time in my life, screwed over. I felt betrayed by you. I felt all the walls spinning around, then everything went black. One of the worst memories in my life, seeing your message to another person and telling them how much you loved them, the same way you told me. Calling them by the nick name that you called me. The worst feeling in this world is being betrayed by the one person you gave your heart to. By that same person you decided to dedicate your entire life to. It's even worse, trying to believe them after you forgave them for it. This is a hard process, to forgive a person and try not to think about that moment. Sometimes the best thing to do is to forgive and let each one go their separate way. Because you can forgive but that pain will live forever within you. I know. I've experienced it, I've lived it, and if I knew what I know now, I would've forgiven them and let them go.

I always thought you noticed my pain. I thought that by you looking into my eyes, you would know how I felt. Unfortunately, that wasn't the case. Not a single drop of understanding came from you. Not a single blink to show a little emotion. Not even a touch of a hand to show, I'm here for you.

CREMATING PAST

I still remember all those days when I had to sit there and drown in my thoughts. See, I always wished I had someone that could understand me and not misinterpret everything I said. What I wished to call home was actually a temporary shelter and what I thought was once love, was also a fabrication. Every day I had to put on my mask to show everyone how happy we seemed, but the reality came during the night and the moments when we were together. God, if looks could kill, I would've been dead many times. It's a shame that I had to spend so many years in search for that day where we would actually look at each other and surrender that ego. Maybe, I should've just walked away when I had the chance at the beginning, but what can I say, I was born to try and see the good in everyone. I don't regret the lesson I learned, my only regret is not allowing my intuition to lead the way.

CARLOS MEDINA

You choked me with all your words,
But that didn't stop me from moving on.

CREMATING PAST

Sometimes you just have to let them go. You can't keep holding on to the thought of " what if ". You can't keep hurting yourself over another person. When that time comes to let them go, don't put blame on yourself, because it's not your fault. You did everything you could do to make things work. It's not an easy step to take, but it's necessary for you, for your heart and for soul.

Never settle for that mediocre love. You deserve better. You deserve that pure rare love. The one that stirs up your soul.

CREMATING PAST

There will be many times when you feel like giving up. Like there is no hope. You might feel your whole inside being ripped apart. You will begin to start looking at everything in a negative way. When this happens, take a step back and take a good look at how far you have come. See all your accomplishments. Understand that through all that past pain and suffering, you're still standing tall.

Perhaps the struggles have been hard. Probably you feel like you have hit rock bottom. You lay down every single night and soak your pillow with tears wondering, why me? What have I done to deserve this? But let me explain something to you, my friend. You are not alone. Many have gone through it, and survived. Your inner strength will rise from within. I promise you that. Soon you will look back and realize that all these obstacles were actually preparing your soul for what the future will bring.

CREMATING PAST

If you gave your heart to someone and they rejected you, don't feel like you did anything wrong. You didn't. They are the ones that didn't see that beauty within you. It's not your fault. Don't you ever think for once it is. You did something that many will never do. You opened up your heart to someone. You allowed them into your most sacred place. And they were just fucking blind to see that sparkling soul of yours. Keep going. Don't stop believing in love. It's out there. Somewhere, someone is looking for that soul that you have. Be patient and allow things to fall into place. Don't rush it. Allow your soul to flow in the winds of this cynical world. You know what you want. Don't settle for less!

Never silence the soul when it desires to scream love.

CREMATING PAST

Every single day, she puts on that smile for you. Doesn't matter what's going on, all you will see is that smile. But you know what? Deep down inside she is hurt. She is hurt because of you. And it's not what you did to her. It's all that you didn't do for her. And it hurts. It fucking hurts her a lot! You forgot she is your partner. She isn't your slave. And you ask yourself now where did you go wrong? Well, I'll tell you. You just stopped seeing her the way you saw her when you first laid eyes on her. There is no more, "hey love," or "have a good day," or "let me help you with this" or just that simple stare in the eyes and allowing her to see that you truly love her. There is no more communication. Social media gets more attention than her. The cuddling stops, now it's her in the bedroom and you're in the living room. Instead of hanging out with the friends, take her out to a nice dinner. Spend a night just the two of you talking about everything. Don't allow the pillow to absorb all her tears, be the man she desired and absorb all her pain. For god sakes, that's your partner in life, cherish her footsteps and watch how beautiful the relationship will be when it's two individuals striving in harmony.

One day it will make sense, the decision you made to find yourself.

CREMATING PAST

We spend our lives desiring something special. We seek this deep romantic love that we know we are capable of giving. And since we know we can give it, we expect to receive it from someone. And we fall for the first one that gives us those butterflies. We fall so deep for them that we do anything for them. Fuck, we dedicate our lives to them. And in return, we get treated like garbage, like complete shit! They hurt us so bad that for some, it takes a long time to heal those wounds. They leave these scars on us. And every day we look at those scars and cry. We cry because we feel the pain inside of them. Just like those scars, we go about doing our regular daily routine with a smile on our face, and to everyone we are all cheery and happy, but no one knows how much pain we have inside. It's a pain that words couldn't describe but feelings can. This pain takes a toll on us. It's well hidden from the public. But god damn does it hurt internally. I promise you something though. There will be one person out there with a powerful force. They will use it to dig up those scars. That powerful force is called deep pure love. You will feel it. You will not understand how they can do it. But everything inside of you will want it. When you come across a rare soul like this, allow their power to manifest within you. Love hurts, but love will heal.

I crucified my ego just to find you.

CREMATING PAST

And if this tear comes down my cheek, just understand it's not from pain. It's one of those tears which comes from a deep place. It's a small drop. But a strong heartfelt one. It's that one of a time tear. It's that tear full of so many emotions and feelings for you. It's the tear of hope, faith and love. The one that drops straight into my soul for that desire of your presence next to me. The one tear that touches your soul and allows you to feel all the love I have within. It's that tear of love.

One day, you will let those guards down. You will feel this warmth within you that it's unexplainable. You will feel love again. You will feel all those broken pieces from your heart aligning once again. You will know how it feels to be loved again. This time, it will be that pure love you've always desired. And for once in your lifetime, you will understand that magical power called love. Cherish it and absorb it.

CREMATING PAST

When someone loves you, they accept you for who you are. They won't try to change you. They will take you in their arms without hesitation. They will protect you and be thero with you.

Within all the pain, she found herself.

CREMATING PAST

Whisper to my soul, speak the language of the unknown. Feel the crown I'm placing around your heart, it's magical, it's precious and full of many colors. It's a symbol of how deep my love is.

It's not healthy to be in a relationship when the soul is empty and not being understood.

CREMATING PAST

I touched her soul with all my love. I gave her the most beautiful memories for her mind to remember. I left prints of my love all over her soul. So when left in the darkest moments, my love will glow within her for eternity.

Some people build this perfect image of their future love, in reality, we must feel the vibrations of a person's soul just to truly get that taste of perfection.

CREMATING PAST

I fell in love with everything hidden in her heart. For they are the treasure that my soul seeks.

I remember that day as if it was yesterday. You said, "I do" with no hesitation. I remember staring at your eyes and wondering if you were ready for this life. By that time I had already lost all my intuition because I always thought that my mind was playing tricks on me. One of the worst feelings in the world is knowing that it should not be a certain way but for some reason, you have to live up to the expectations of others. But who cared about feelings, when I thought I had the world with you by my side. The first couple of months were beautiful. No arguments, no worries and no heartache. As time went by, we drifted apart. You gave your attention to a tablet while I stood in the living room watching television. No more date nights and slowly the communication was gone. By that time, that love that I felt began to fade away. Four years later, I felt like a stranger in my own home. The person that I married left the marriage a while back. We were attached by the last name, by a paper that legally meant something but emotionally meant nothing. Yet people still asked me what I did wrong. But the reality is, we were two individuals living a fabricated life. Even when you left, I still tried. I tried so much to rekindle our marriage. But how can I rekindle something that had no depth? How? How can I ask you to stay, when you already left a long time ago? But I understand. I know that it was all the little things that kept piling up on you. I cannot put all the blame on you. I do thank you for the beautiful moments that we had, even the bad ones. Because of you, because of what we experienced, I found the path that I was meant to walk. Thank you.

CREMATING PAST

There are echoes of love, floating in the darkest alleys of your soul .

I had to recognize, that in order for me to find a soul that could understand my depth, I needed to dig deep within myself and acknowledge the powerful soul that's burning inside.

CREMATING PAST

Can I get on my knees and spill all my tears? Can I surrender my heart and trust that you will not live in fear? Perhaps it's true, actions do speak more than words, but I know that my soul will speak to you and understand everything that everyone couldn't comprehend. Just let go, and feel the magical tunes.

The cravings, yearnings and the desires are what she felt when his presence took over her soul.

CREMATING PAST

I remember the day when you said, "I'm leaving." Those words will forever exist inside me. Although I forgave you, the pain will live in me. See, to me it was more than just a part of my life spent with you. It was my dedication and loyalty to you. It was me giving you everything I had, because I truly loved you. I look back now and see all the signs that were there from the start, but for some reason, I was blind and deeply in love. It's amazing, you give everything to a person and all of a sudden, it's all gone. It becomes a memory and a painful event. While that person is out there experimenting with life, we are here wondering what we did so wrong to deserve this. I have learned to take it all in, to realize that these are lessons in this life. No one was ever given a life that was easy. But I just look back and wonder, what if I had listened to all those people and my gut feeling that told me not to do it. I wonder that sometimes.

And although pain draws a dotted line across my mind. I promise you, I can let them all go.

CREMATING PAST

I set you free. Free like a butterfly. You now can spread your wings and take on this world like nobody else can. I gave you my love knowing it would help heal your scars. While we drowned together in depths, I decided to keep sinking in it, for it was the only place I knew no one else can come in and interfere.

Close your mind, open your soul. Allow me to see the rest of you.

CREMATING PAST

I cry every morning as the sun rises, knowing that a new day starts without your presence.

My soul cries knowing, that no matter what it does, you will never be by my side.

CREMATING PAST

Sometimes you feel lonely even with the person right next to you.

She lost several pieces of her mask every time, just to truly find her pure soul.

CREMATING PAST

Pure feelings and emotions from the soul. That's what made me give her my all.

I value more what I feel. Not what I see.

CREMATING PAST

Wait for me. I'm almost there. I know it's hard. But just wait for me. Have patience my dear. The time will come when our souls will unite. It's been a long journey. This I know for sure. I have walked through the valleys of life and encountered many obstacles. But before I even stopped to think I realized that my path was leading to you. And as time passes, I'm just learning. I'm learning to build within what you expect from me. Wait for me.

When you believe and trust in the powerful force of love, you will never have to doubt.

CREMATING PAST

If I gave you my love, would you cherish it? Would you understand that what I'm giving you is something with pure depth? Something that I never gave another soul in this world. It's fragile. Please take care of it.

Would you give me the time that's needed to assemble my heart for you? I promise it won't take long. It'll be crafted by heaven with a touch of the unknown. It's been a while that it has worked properly. But for you, I'll make sure it's a masterpiece.

CREMATING PAST

Just come rescue my soul from this hurtful world.

I may have felt the pain of many. I'm probably the story you read so many times about: the girl with a fucked-up past. I've given my heart in full before to others and in return, I just got shattered pieces of it back. Cut my wings, bruise my mind, but I'll promise you one thing, no one will never get the chance to destroy my soul.

CREMATING PAST

Don't worry, she won't drown. She knows exactly how to survive in depths.

All it takes is for you to believe. Believe in yourself and transform all that negativity into positivity. And watch how beautiful the outcome will be.

CREMATING PAST

A male who echoes your love is the replacement to all your doubts.

You deserve better, and you know it. For some reason you're stuck in the, "why me?" Why haven't I found a person that will love me the way I love? Why must I go through all this bullshit in life? Why does it seem like I'm the only one trying to survive in this crazy world? Guess what? You are not alone. Many others are going through the same problems. You need to understand that many of your problems truly are fixable. You want to attract the best soul out there, you must be the best soul out there. Whatever you send out to the universe is exactly what you shall get in return. You want a pure soul? Be a pure soul. You want deep passionate love? Be the passionate person. And no, I'm not talking about your physical appearance, I'm talking about what's underneath all those layers. The beautiful treasure in your soul. Bring it forth, be patient and watch the miracles from the unknown unfold right in front of you. It's a long process, but the outcome is eternal peace and love.

CREMATING PAST

You deserve nothing less than pure love. Remember that!

Not many can handle a powerful soul like mine. And yes, I can live with that.

CREMATING PAST

It's not a felony to blowtorch the memories of my past, in order, to find that eternal soul that carries the love I desire.

There is always that thin line between two powerful souls. It's invisible yet there. It's not imaginary but magical. It has the strength to separate them and bring them together. Not many can see it, but these two can sure feel it. If only the past can be put aside and fight the hesitations, that line can be used to unite them and build that balance between them.

They say to show love to a woman, you must meet up to her standards. I say to love a woman, you must be able to be vulnerable to her. You must fall in love with her every single day. You must feel her whole interior. You must be the security for her. You need to understand that she wants to have a future with you. You have to pay attention to all the little details about her. Being with this precious soul isn't about showing off, trust me, she prefers a night at home relaxing and drinking wine. She prefers just the two of you talking about all the crazy things that go on in your head. Don't think she won't care. She does care, and cares a lot. Just treat her with respect and don't expect her to change for you. Love her the way you found her, love her the way she is. And if you don't understand some of her thoughts, ask her to explain in more depth. She won't mind. Caress her, adore her, and above all the things mentioned, love her beyond eternity. She isn't perfect and neither are you. Take good care of her, or someone else will.

To understand and feel the love of another soul, you must be able to give in to the powerful unknown and trust your soul.

CREMATING PAST

I brought tears to your eyes, just so you know that pureness still exist. I reconstructed the whole alphabet, just to make sure it fits perfectly into your soul. I opened up all my wounds, just to assure you that we all have a fucked up past. You have fought all the battles of your thoughts at night and continue to experience many dejavú of the synchronization of our souls. Close your eyes, experience the beautiful powers of the unknown, and for once, allow yourself to be loved.

And if I could turn back the hands of time, I would have found you many lifetimes ago. I would chisel my words on stones just so the future US would look back and know how pure our love was. Fast forwarding through time, we finally reach the destination where we hold hands and carve our hearts on the beautiful oak tree. We become elites playing hide and seek and drift away into our dreams. We live the fairytales of love and create the mysteries that we each seek. Crossing paths again, finally, we reach what was hidden for so long, our souls united by the magic that runs deep within. Take my hand, and don't look back. We are both standing at the edge of forever. It's time to spread our wings and learn how to fly as one.

CREMATING PAST

Just close your eyes and be the center piece of my soul. Imagination runs wild, but I'll be there to caress all your thoughts. None of us are wrong in taking our time now, for we have sacrificed our lives for the past.

We will cross paths with many individuals on a daily basis. We will fall in love with them for many reasons. Some will just give us a taste of their love, others will actually show us that they do understand us in many ways. We will fall so hard for them. For we will finally feel what it's like to be understood and cherished. And those that give us that taste of love, they are the ones that are passing by to open our eyes. They are the ones that will make sure we understand that not everyone is the same from what we have experienced. And that's ok. We should thank them for giving us a part of their gift. Those that do decide to stay, those are the rare ones. Those are the ones that are just like us. They felt pain, they suffered, they know what it is to be lonely. Those rare individuals are a reflection of ourselves in the mirror. And you will feel so much for them. Because it's exactly what you felt all this time. Those are the unique souls that will open our souls again. They will give us this deep passionate love that we never experienced before. If by any chance you cross paths with one, absorb all their energy. Believe me, they have this beautiful vibe that you will feel it miles apart. Show them that pure side of you. Watch from a distance and you'll see that they care about you. They are truly the rare souls nowadays. If you find one, don't let them go. Hold on to them. You just might have found what they call a soulmate.

CREMATING PAST

I bleed love, for my soul desires to feel it.

I loved you so much, that I had to let you go. It was never my intention to hurt you. I knew all along you would fix yourself the way you wanted. I will never reduce the amount of love and passion I hold within, and after all this time I finally understand, that our views in life were totally different. No regrets, no sadness. I wish you the best in love and life. And I'll forever cherish the moments we crossed paths.

CREMATING PAST

I don't care what people say, but there will always be better. Now it's just up to you, will you wait for better? Or will you make what you have better? The choice is always yours.

Para amarte con todo mi corazón, tuve que dejar todas mis lágrimas del pasado y rendir mi alma para ti.

CREMATING PAST

To love you with all my heart, I needed to drain my soul of its tears for the past.

CARLOS MEDINA

To love you, I had to let go of all my past and grow titanium wings, just to carry your soul into our future.

CREMATING PAST

You are entitled to a pure love, never settle for that recycled bullshit!

Allow me to kiss away those tears from your soul, my whole life I was known for absorbing pain. Let it all out on me and watch how beautiful this healing stage can be.

CREMATING PAST

Never allow your soul to be trapped in the minds of others.

CARLOS MEDINA

It's ok to fall, it's ok to cry and it's ok to feel deeply. But never stay down, never allow the mind to rule your soul and don't you ever give up!

CREMATING PAST

Meet me halfway, meet me at the forest of pain, underneath the tree of life. Stand there and close your eyes, feel my presence right behind you, feel the warmth of my soul caressing you, just take my hand and drift away with me into a place that beauty shines bright, come with me into the unknown.

You don't need to have fancy things in life to demonstrate what you are worth.

CREMATING PAST

Just have a beautiful soul, that's something money can't buy.

We met many eternities, centuries and lifetimes ago. We crossed paths and tasted each other's hearts. Stimulated each other's minds like no other person. I will find you again, this time, I'll make pure love to your soul. I'll strip all your fears away and hold on to you forever and ever, until we reincarnate. You'll be my butterfly and I'll be your rose. Together, we will bring happiness and joy to rest of our garden.

CREMATING PAST

It's ok to cry, the soul also needs its cleansing.

She isn't perfect, she is far from being perfect. But she strives daily to be close to it as possible. She is that girl that's always smiling. And although her past has fucked her over many times, she'll keep that smile on her face daily. She does it for she believes that no one should know her private life. And it's beautiful to all her friends, but deep down inside she is the one that's hurt. See, what we don't see is, she soaks up her pillow every night wondering what tomorrow will bring. She wants to find someone to love and to share a future with, but she is scared. She is scared that someone will come and take advantage of her. She is scared that someone will replicate what her past partner did. And you can't blame her. Living in this world full of evil individuals, she must be cautious about everything. She will find that person. She will find that true soulmate. And she will fall in love again. Just with a better understanding of her soul and its depth. For now, she will seek what the eyes cannot see. She will search for that purity within a person.

CREMATING PAST

She will not surrender her soul until she finds the person that surrenders his.

She never needed a spotlight. She shined brighter than a million suns.

CREMATING PAST

In case this is the last time we speak. Just remember I gave you my soul. And if by any chance you decide to come look for me, I'll be patiently waiting at the edge of forever.

How depressing it is to see couples and see the sadness in her eyes.

CREMATING PAST

Catch her drift, feel her vibe and understand what she is looking for is beyond your understanding.

We drifted apart without a reason. We hid well in our shells hoping that the emotions were temporary. We denied everything we felt, for it was hard to understand the depth of pure love. We searched in others what we felt from each other, hoping that someone would replicate what we truly desired. I crossed paths with many just to feel again, but not one person can reach in and stir up my soul. Memories are what's left of the beautiful view through your eyes. I give a lot of power to my imagination just to see the future with you by my side. Cut the cord, burn the bridge, but one thing is for sure, you'll forever be the rose that grew in my soul.

How can my soul bypass the glimpses from your thoughts? When in this imagination the strokes of my brush are just touching the curves of your skin. Two individuals from time zones apart, creating beautiful masterpieces from the taste of each other's hearts. Loose your judgement, bubble wrap my desires and pull me close. Perhaps I'll meet your madness, perhaps I won't always understand, but once you taste my thoughts, you will feel how strong my soul can adore. Is this what they call a high? Or an elevation? Call it what you want, but seeing the world through your eyes is actually capturing every moment within blinks from my third eye.

I stitched up my heart with the love she gave me.

CREMATING PAST

It didn't matter which mask she used. For what I saw was hidden deep within.

Release all the echoes of your past, for I am here now, creating all the cravings and yearnings of your soul.

CREMATING PAST

Never give up! Never stop believing! Trust in the powers you have! See things with your soul instead of your eyes, and watch the beauty you will attract.

I looked into your soul. I saw something hidden in for such a long time. I wanted to touch it. I wanted to feel it. There is something about it that makes me want to live the rest of my life exploring it. It's pure. It's sacred. It's honest. It's beauty that so many failed to see. It's magical. It's hypnotizing. It's alluring. I want to polish it and wear it around my heart. It's felt deeply. It's unknown. But it's powerful. And I'm attracted to power. It's mysterious. And it can't be defined. But we both know what's held deep inside. We opened the door to our dreams. We knew that the other guarded the gateway to reality. It couldn't be an easy process, for we knew the outcome when things come easy. We broke into each other's thoughts without using tactical force. How could it be? We questioned. But in reality, we knew that we couldn't interfere with the powerful unknown.

CREMATING PAST

You are perfect just like you are. You have this unique gift that many will never understand. Don't you ever try to change for anyone.

Speak to me in the unknown language, for my soul is ready to love you.

CREMATING PAST

Don't allow anyone to touch you, until they have given you all the authority to their soul.

I wanted to take it a step further, I didn't want to hear about her past and pain. Not needed. For I felt it and lived it all. I wanted to talk to her about her future and what she saw. I wanted to know what she wanted. What she loved. I wanted to remanufacture this old soul to her requests. I wanted it to fit perfectly into her.

ABOUT THE AUTHOR

Carlos Medina was born and raised in the Bronx, New York. He is known for sharing most of his talent on Instagram and Facebook. His writing began three years ago after a divorce from a five-year marriage. By sharing his past pain and healing, he began captivating his readers with his words as he has experienced different facets of life and has the ability to show you the vulnerability of your- self through his words. Traveling through the deepest crevices of your mind, exploring the passages of your heart, you'll be able to explore the depths of your soul and experience memories in ways you never did before.

CONNECT WITH THE AUTHOR

Carlos Medina

Website: magesoul.com
Email: magesoul@outlook.com
Instagram: magesoul
Facebook: magesoul
Twitter: magesoul

ALSO AVAILABLE BY THE AUTHOR

WWW.MAGESOUL.COM

ALSO AVAILABLE BY THE AUTHOR

   WWW.MAGESOUL.COM

ALSO AVAILABLE BY THE AUTHOR

 WWW.MAGESOUL.COM

AUTHORS:
Myke Duarte Carlos
Carlos Medina

AVAILABLE

 WWW.MAGESOUL.COM

FEBRUARY 2019

 WWW.MAGESOUL.COM

JULY 2019

WWW.MAGESOUL.COM

CHRISTMAS EVE 2019
LUMINOUS SOUL SERIES
By Carlos Medina

FOUR BOOKS

ONE PRICE

GREAT GIFT

WWW.MAGESOUL.COM

Magesoul Publishing is now accepting submissions from writers in the future who wish to get their book published through this corporation.

Submit or send inquiries to:
submissions@magesoulpublishing.com

www.ingramcontent.com/pod-product-compliance
Lightning Source LLC
Chambersburg PA
CBHW020424010526
44118CB00010B/401